5

SHINY AND HER WARDROBE OF VIRTUES

LOVE

STRONG FEELINGS OF AFFECTION

BY

Sukanya Shah

First published by Birch Books 2020

ISBN - 978-81-949495-9-6

Email : books.birch@gmail.com

To Adyana.
My first. My all.
May you always be more.

From the Author's Desk

Cossetted in our homes during the thick of the Covid-19 pandemic, I made every effort to keep my toddler happy and engaged. It made me wonder about the true legacy in learning that my child will bequeath. I cannot wait to pass on this treasure of a less than perfect world to her... one that will astonish her most often, teach her most definitely and hold her to two constants—challenge and change.

Shiny And Her Wardrobe Of Virtues was born of this sentiment. Shiny is a spritely little girl who owns a magical wardrobe, with virtuous items that on adorning, change her world view...virtues that go beyond the classroom and make her feel happy and whole.

I enjoyed writing these stories of gratitude, kindness, confidence, patience and love...but more so, I enjoyed diving into these most beautiful emotions and feelings with my child.

I hope you do too.

Love,
Sukanya.

It was the start of summer, Shiny was pleased,
Into the lemonade jar, juicy lemons she squeezed.

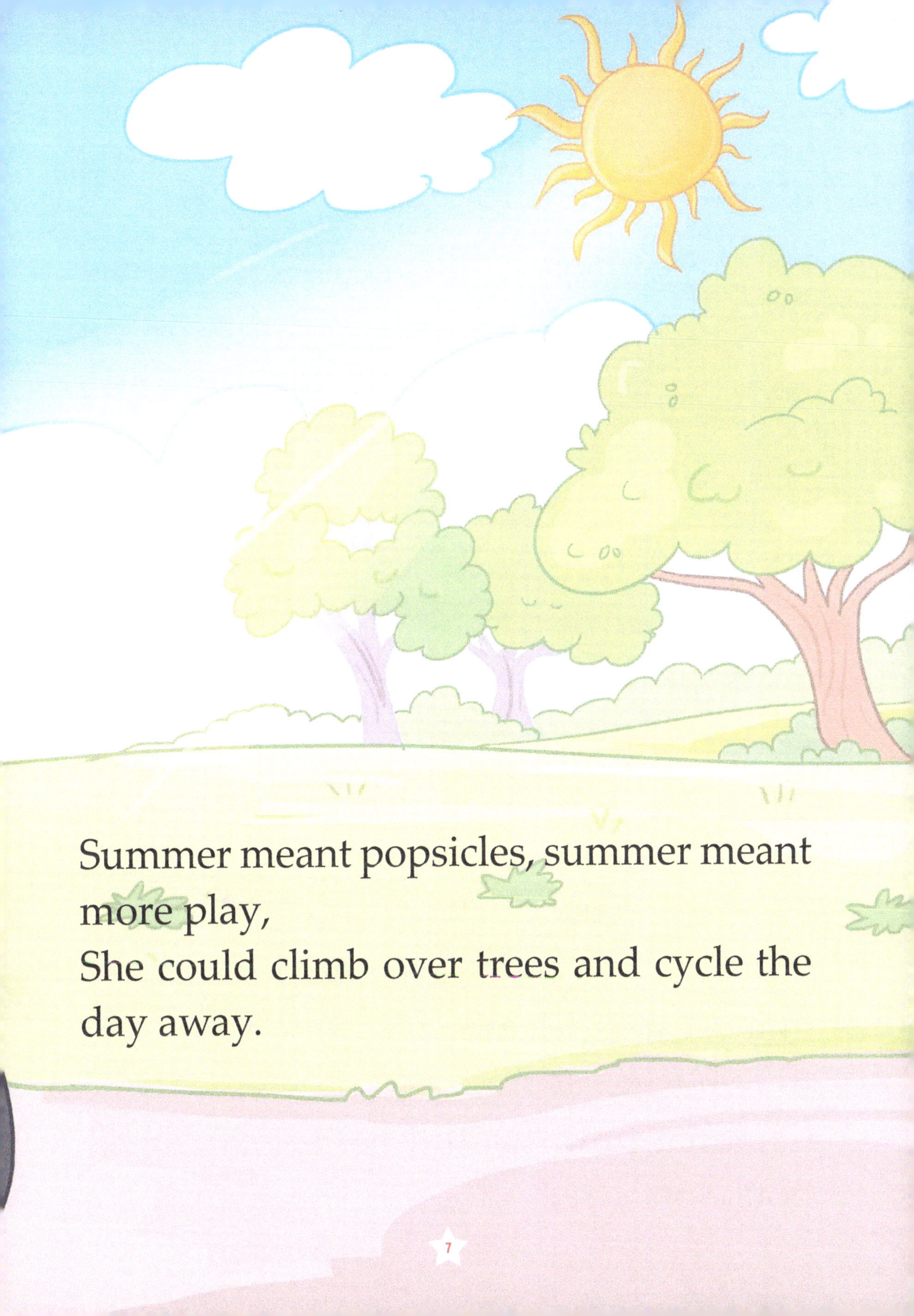

Summer meant popsicles, summer meant more play,
She could climb over trees and cycle the day away.

Shiny carried lemonade, she went over to Bobby's.
Oh what fun it would be, to play in his house on a tree!

They climbed and they crawled, onto the tree top.
She hung with one arm, Bobby said, "Shiny stop!"

She lost her strong grip, she sweated and frowned,
Shiny screamed for help, but fell hard on her crown.

Bobby ran to help her, the mummies came scuttling out,
They rushed her to the doctor, Shiny had a blackout.

The doctor revived her, as she slowly opened her eyes,
This head injury was painful, Shiny winced with the slightest noise.

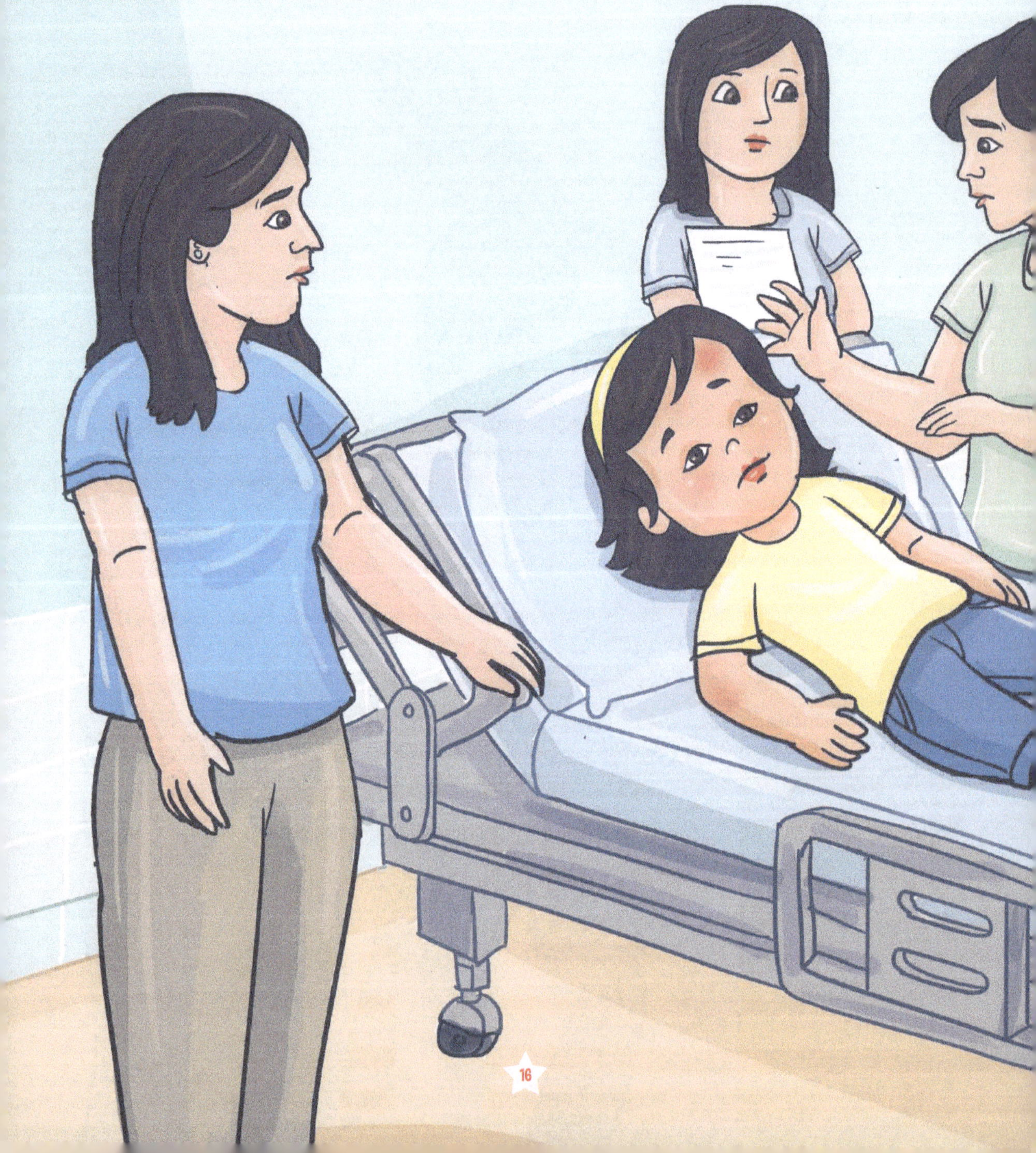

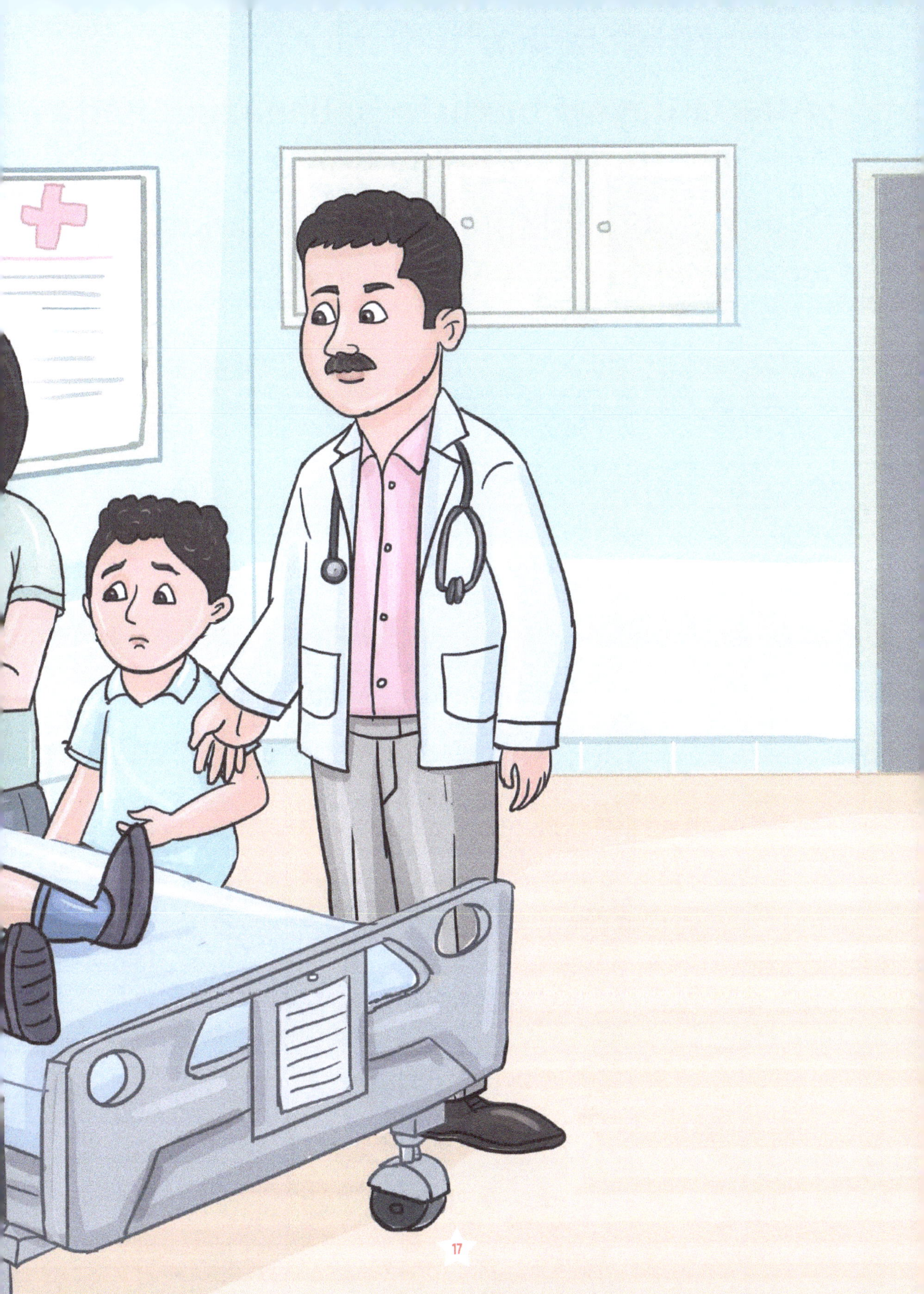

After a day of medicines, bandages and ice, Mummy took Shiny home.
Shiny snuggled into her love blanket, she could neither play nor roam.

Her bump was rather painful, Daddy iced the pain away.
Mummy read her storybooks, they took care of her all day.

STORY
AUG

She felt much better soon, in her warm blanket of love.

Mummy and Daddy's care, was her blessing from above.

AUG
10

"Is this the love they speak of, in stories and in song?"
"Is this what makes one's heart swell, with a feeling that's so warm?"

AUG
10

Her blanket of love felt cosy, her blanket of love felt safe.
Much like Mummy's kisses, and a lot like Daddy's embrace.

Five days went by, in the blink of an eye. The medicines were done, "I'm all the better!" Shiny cried.

ON
NDAY
AUG
11

They went to visit the doctor, to check her bump and scar.
He said, "Shiny's recovered, she's come through like a star!"

"I feel like my old self" said Shiny, "thank you kind Doctor".
More than the medicines, it's love that made me better!

Shiny felt true love, her blanket shimmered grand.
This true and terrific feeling, she sure did understand.

Talking points for parents:

- Ask your child to make a list of the people and pets they love most.

- Ask your child what they think may be the meaning of love and write it down, you could tell them what they said years later as a sweet memory.

- Talk to your child about different manifestations of love: The love between parents and a child, the love of a sibling, the love one feels for a grandparent, the love between friends, etc.

- Discuss with your child the various ways in which they could express their love. For example share a toy with a friend, help a grandparent with a chore, etc.

- Help your child make love cards or notes for the top three people on their list and make one for your child too!